Along the Advent Road
Inspirational Ideas

Nick Harding

kevin mayhew

First published in 2004 by

KEVIN MAYHEW LTD
Buxhall, Stowmarket, Suffolk, IP14 3BW
E-mail: info@kevinmayhewltd.com

KINGSGATE PUBLISHING INC
1000 Pannell Street, Suite G, Columbia, MO 65201
E-mail: sales@kingsgatepublishing.com

9 8 7 6 5 4 3 2 1 0

ISBN 1 84417 279 1
Catalogue No. 1500715

Edited by Graham Harris
Cover design by Angela Selfe
Typesetting by Richard Weaver

Printed and bound in Great Britain

Contents

Introduction

Advent is really a journey. The journey takes us from the bleakness of late autumn and winter into the brightness of the Christmas celebrations. It takes us from the sense of gloom we feel inside into the smiles and happiness of gatherings. More importantly, Advent leads us to the great celebrations that mark the birth of Jesus.

As we travel the Advent road we have in mind the others whose journeys are significant at Advent. We remember the shepherds, working in their remote fields and then rushing down the hillsides to see the new-born baby. We think of the wise men, journeying long distances possibly over many months in order to worship. And we can't forget Mary and Joseph themselves, walking from home to that strange and hectic city of Bethlehem.

The Advent journey carried out by the 'Magi', men of wealth, wisdom and authority, has been the subject of debate for generations. It may well have been that they arrived to visit Jesus many days or weeks after the birth, and some translations suggest that by that stage Mary, Joseph and the baby were staying in a house. It is certainly one of the many myths of the Christmas story that the wise men and shepherds were physically present at the same time. Some churches remember the visit of the wise men on Epiphany in early January.

The fact is that we do not know, and to get too tied up with when things may or may not have happened can cause us to lose out also on the essence of the story. The essence is that as men of power and money from foreign lands visited and worshipped we are reminded that Christ is for all people, from all places and all backgrounds.

Most schools and many churches include the wise men in their services and activities as they approach Christmas, and therefore they feature in this selection of ideas.

The ideas in this book can be used as 'pick and mix', with a combination of games and activities, talks and prayers to suit all situations and time available.

This collection of games, ideas, activities, talks and prayers will help schools, classes, groups and congregations walk the Advent road together.

Games and Activities

These games and activities can be used in small or large groups, churches or schools. Some are discussion-starters, some are games that include a few people, and others are things that everyone can do.

The rich get going

You will need: paper, pencils

Imagine you have plenty of money, and you are about to go on a very long journey. You don't know how long the journey will be, or what you may find at the end of it. You are living 2000 years ago, so you have no cars, aeroplanes or trains to travel on . . . just a camel! List ten things that you would like to take with you.

Telling journeys

Get into pairs. One of you is a wise man, and you are about to set off following the large, bright star in the sky. The other is a friend of the wise man who thinks he is a bit mad deciding to just go off following a star! Talk to each other, discussing this strange situation.

Week by week

You will need: Long sheets of paper for each person, scissors, pens, glue sticks

Each week of Advent ask each person to draw a few scenes of all that you have seen and done. Cut each one out and stick it on a longer piece of paper. At the end of Advent look at the sheet of paper, and spend some time reflecting on the journey through Advent.

Pack a bag

You will need: torch, map, coat, blanket, rucksack, compass, clothes, and other items for journeys

The wise men probably didn't take lots of things with them on their journey, and it must have been difficult to decide what to take and what to leave behind. With the group, decide on which items are the most important. This could be done by clapping or cheering for each item, and deciding which are most important. Pack the most important things into the bag.

Route finders

Split the group into smaller groups, and ask them to discuss the following questions:

How do you find your way to work/school/home?

What things do you use to find your way to new places?

Who do you trust to help you find your way?

How does God help us find our way through life?

Starry ideas

You will need: paper stars, pencils

Hand out a paper four-pointed star for each person. Explain that the wise men set off on a journey to something very special – they were going to find a new King. Ask each person to write on each of the four points of their own star where they would really like to go to and what very special things they would like to see.

The write way

You will need: flipchart, pens

Put some flipchart paper on the floor in the middle of the group or stick it up on the wall. Ask the group to consider all the feelings that the wise men may have had when setting out on their uncertain journey. Remind them that the wise men were probably rich and powerful, but also may have had homes, families, and responsibilities. Then invite them to write up words that may be how the wise men felt onto the flipchart paper. Start them off with the following suggestions:

Happy	Excited
Worried	Nervous

Finding the way

You will need: a map, a person, a large star

Ask the group who they would most like to follow to somewhere they have never been before. Would they feel happiest following a person who says they know the way? Would they be more confident if they had a map to guide them? Would they be pleased to follow a star at night? Ask them to get into groups of three or four and talk about which guidance they prefer.

The East

You will need: a flipchart or whiteboard and pens

Work with the group in devising a short acrostic poem about the wise men based on the word EAST. An example would be:

Everything left behind,
Always watching the night sky.
Stars shine, one shines brighter
Telling the way to go.

Let me know!

You will need: three volunteers

Mention the wise men calling to see King Herod, and Herod's request that they should return and tell him where the baby is. Ask for three volunteers to say the following phrases in turn, and everyone else is to decide who makes it sound most genuine:

> *Come back and tell me*
> *I want to worship the new King*
> *Let me know what happens*

Way to go

You will need: a blindfold, two volunteers

The wise men had to trust the star, and follow it wherever it took them. Ask one volunteer to wear a blindfold, and the other one to give verbal instructions to help find his/her way from one place to another without walking into anything.

Expectations

In small groups ask everyone to try to put themselves in the position of being a visitor to the stable where Jesus was born. What might they have expected? Use these questions to help:

How different from what they may have expected was the stable?
How do they think they would have felt?
Would they have been disappointed or amazed?

Bringing gifts

You will need: pieces of paper soaked in perfume, pieces of small gold paper or foil, a large bowl or basket at the front

Hide the perfumed paper and gold foil around the room/church. Ask the people to imagine that they are coming to worship the new-born baby. They should then search for one item (ether perfumed paper or gold foil) and quietly bring it up to place in the bowl or basket.

Taking time

You will need: a 5p piece for everyone

Advent is about having time for thinking and concentrating on the coming birth of Jesus. Give each person a five pence piece at the beginning of Advent, and challenge them to spend five minutes a day thinking about the coming birth of Jesus.

Put aside

You will need: a bin bag for everyone

Give all the people a bin bag. Talk through how Advent can be a time to clear out the rubbish and make room for Jesus. Ask them to go through their belongings – games, toys, clothes, books, etc. – and put those that they do not want into the bin bag. You may know a local charity or agency that will be able to use the discarded items.

Dream future

You will need: thought bubbles on paper, pens

Give out the thought bubbles, one for each person. Ask them to write or draw into the thought bubble the best future they can imagine. Then remind them of the future that Mary and Joseph may have imagined . . . until Mary discovered God's plan for her.

Gabriel's message

You will need: a large card with the word 'fear', and another one with 'delight' on them

Ask two volunteers to hold each sign, one on each side at the front. Then read out the following phrases, asking everyone to point at either 'fear' or 'delight' depending on how they think Mary must have felt.

An angel appeared to Mary

The angel told Mary not to be afraid

Mary was confused by the news that she was given

Mary realised she was going to have a special baby

The angel told Mary not to be afraid

She heard that her son would be very special

She realised that there is nothing that God cannot do

Mary promised to do all that God wanted

How happy!

You will need: two volunteers

Mary was happy to do what God said, and Elizabeth said to her: 'How happy you are to believe that the Lord's message to you will come true!' Play a simple word association game based on the word 'happy'. Ask each person to say a different word in turn about things that make them feel happy, without hesitation or repetition. The winner is the player who manages to keep going longest.

Do you believe?

Mary believed the amazing news that she was to have a baby, and that God would be with her. Remind everyone that we are called to believe all that God says and offers to do for us. Ask them to stop and think for a few minutes about the things they really believe that God does for them.

Don't be afraid

You will need: a sheet of paper on the wall, pens

The angel told Mary not to be afraid. Even in Advent we may have things that make us feel afraid. We may be worried about getting everything ready for Christmas, or worried about singing or performing at Christmas concerts or services. Invite everyone to write on the sheet things that they sometimes feel afraid of, and remember Gabriel's words to Mary.

Are you ready?

Ask the group to stand. Ask them to move around and ask people around them the following question. Give everyone one minute per question:

Are you ready for parties and celebrations?
Are you ready to receive presents and gifts?
Are you ready to give presents and gifts?
Are you ready to eat and drink?
Are you ready to meet Jesus?

What's in the letter?

You will need: three letters in envelopes (details below), three volunteers

1. *You have just been told some shocking news*
2. *You have to go on a long, hard journey*
3. *You have been given some exciting news*

Each of the volunteers is given a letter to read. In turn they then act out what the letter is telling them. The other people should try to guess what the message is. Mary and Joseph did not get a letter like our modern letters telling them to go to Jerusalem, but they would have been told, and they had to do it.

Step by step

You will need: A set of nine cards: three with '0', three with '1', and three with '2'; two volunteers

Mary and Joseph had a long walk of more than 50 miles, and it would have probably taken them quite a few days. This is a walk that is much shorter! The volunteers have to choose a card from those you have made and are holding face-down. They can then step forward the distance that the card says towards a chosen point. You may want to give a prize to the winner!

Donkey or not?

Small groups should discuss and try to decide whether they think Mary rode to Jerusalem on a donkey, as legend tells us. Here are a few things to help:

> *There is no mention of the donkey in the gospels*
> *Mary and Joseph were probably not rich enough to own a donkey*
> *A donkey would have needed food, which would have cost money*
> *We will never actually know, but it is not likely that Mary rode on a donkey.*

Looking forward

You will need: four volunteers, a whistle

Ask the volunteers to come to the front and stand in a line. They must each talk continuously in turn for 30 seconds on what they are looking forward to during Advent as they think about Christmas. If they hesitate or stop they are out of the game. Once the time is up blow the whistle.

Advent lights

This is a quiz for two teams. Taking a team at a time, give the following clues and award points for guessing the answer.

Street lights:	*These are on roads* *They are sometimes orange*
Stars:	*They are a long way away* *They lit the way for special visitors*
Torches:	*They are held in the hand* *They contain batteries*
Candles:	*They contain a string* *They sometimes flicker or go out*
Angel lights:	*They lit up the fields of sheep* *Heavenly creatures glowed*

Crowded town

Mary and Joseph arrived in Bethlehem to find that the town was full of other people looking for somewhere to stay. Ask everyone to stand, and then move around amongst each other asking the question: 'Have you a room for us?' Once they have done this for a few minutes point out the creeping sense of sadness and despair Mary and Joseph must have felt as they tried to find somewhere to stay.

Mapping our way

You will need: small pieces of map

Ask everyone to close their eyes and imagine that they are walking towards Christmas. Ask them to get into pairs and discuss all the things that they need to do on their journey, and the challenges of getting everything ready in time. Then ask them to open their eyes and look at the map. Ask them to identify fields, woods or parks on the map where they can be quiet. God wants us all to find that space and quiet this Advent.

Rocky road

You will need: if possible, large pictures of roads or paths of varied standard

Hold up each picture or describe different roads in turn, and ask the people to think about the question: 'Which experiences of life are like this road?'

> Rocky road (troubles, unsettled, challenges)
> Smooth road (God's presence, easy decisions)
> Narrow road (difficult times, clear way that should be followed)
> Junction (decisions, choices, not sure what to do)

Ready for the birth

You will need: a baby or baby doll, a flipchart and pen

If possible interview the parent/s of a recently born baby, asking them what they did to get ready for the birth of the child, and write those things onto the flipchart. If there are no suitable parents available ask for suggestions instead. Then cross out the things which Mary and Joseph did not have the opportunity to do or get ready before the birth of Jesus.

What's a good job?

Ask everyone to stand. Then explain that if the job you mention is one they would like to do they should stand, if they are not sure they should crouch, but if it is a job they definitely would not want then they should sit.

Teacher	Doctor
Church leader	Shopkeeper
Innkeeper	Police officer
Lorry driver	Shepherd
King	Servant

Shepherds speak

You will need: a volunteer

Explain that in the time that Jesus was born the job of being a shepherd was not popular. They worked long hours, were in danger from wild animals, and often didn't have much to do with other people in their home town or village. The volunteer should imagine that they are a shepherd, and answer your questions about the job without saying the word 'sheep'. Questions could include:

What is the job like?

What are sheep used for?

What hours do you work?

What do you look after?

What do those animals sound like?

How do you make sure they are all safe?

Get ready, go

You will need: two sets of clothes (coats, hats, gloves, Wellington boots, etc), two volunteers

The angels came to visit the shepherds, and very soon the shepherds were in a hurry to journey down to find the new-born baby. This is a race for the two volunteers to dress in the sets of clothes and run to the 'stable' (a point chosen by you!).

Peace to . . .

You will need: Post-it notes, pencils

Read the words the angels said to the shepherds from Luke 2:14. Then ask everyone to write on a Post-it note the names of people who they would like to experience God's peace.

Quick kneel

You will need: music on CD or tape that can be stopped quickly, pillows or cushions, some (fit) volunteers

This is a kneeling variation of the traditional game musical bumps. Remind the group that all people were willing to kneel at the manger once they realised how special the baby Jesus was. Shepherds and kings kneeled at the same point to worship him. Then play the music, stopping it at random and encouraging the people to kneel onto the cushions or pillows as quickly as possible.

On the run

The shepherds ran down the lanes and tracks from their fields to find the baby in the town of Bethlehem. Read out the following phrases, asking anyone to suggest the missing words or phrases in the sentences that the shepherds may have said:

> *I was .... when the sky lit up*
> *The angels were really ....*
> *What do you think they meant about .... ?*
> *I wonder how the .... are?*
> *The singing was really ....*
> *I wonder what we will find when we get to ....*
> *I've got .... as a gift for the child.*

Arriving

The Advent road led Mary and Joseph to the stable, the wise men to the stable, and the shepherds to the stable. Invite everyone to think of a word that the shepherds or wise men may have said when they finally reached the end of the road. Then after counting to three ask everyone to say, shout and whisper the word they thought of.

Games and **Activities**

Talks

These talks can be delivered by an individual or a team of people. They will need to be adapted to your own situation, and could be split over two sessions.

Wise people journey

The wise men went to see Jesus, and in this talk we examine what their actions can teach us today. The three headings for each section can be used as a repeated response, with everyone repeating it each time it is said.

Find out

The wise men had to prepare in order to set off on their journey, and were busy trying to find out about the stars. They had been studying old writings and wanted to find out what was happening above them, looking at the planets and stars in the sky. They knew from all that they had studied that they had discovered something that was a once-in-a-lifetime sight – a star that would lead to a new King. They had to find out a lot of information before they could set off on their journey.

What are you ready to find out this Advent? Are you ready to find out how much Jesus came to make life good for you? Are you going to find out more about what Christmas really means? To find out about Jesus has got to be better for us all than finding out about parties, pantomimes or even presents!

Keep going

It is a hard journey, but the wise men just keep going. They could only travel far at night, because in the day they wouldn't be able to keep going as they couldn't see the star. They may have been cold, too – because although it was probably baking hot in the day, night time could be very cold indeed. And have you ever tried riding on a camel for a few minutes, let alone day after day? Having sore bums must have made it very difficult to keep going! Then they met with Herod, and although he pretended to want to help them, they must have known that his welcoming smile was not as friendly as it seemed, and this may have made them nervous. But they knew it was right to keep going, whatever happened, and however painful or tiring it was.

As Christmas gets nearer it gets more and more difficult to think about Jesus in all the rush and busyness of Advent. We have to keep going, getting things ready and buying presents. But we should also keep going in our aim to keep Jesus at the centre and find out more about all he has to offer us.

Come to worship

The wise men were determined to follow the star that would lead them to the new King. They didn't want to find the new King in order to be famous or to better themselves . . . they wanted to see the child in order to come to worship him. They knew that the star was an invitation to them to come to worship, and they wanted to come to worship the new King. Herod was scared, and said he wanted to come to worship himself, but really he only wanted to kill the baby. The shepherds had come to worship, and now it was the turn of the wise men. And as they knelt before Jesus all the tiredness, dirt and aches from their long journey faded away – they had come to worship at last, and that was all that mattered.

And so, if we find out more about Jesus and keep on remembering what Advent is all about, we are invited to come to worship. We worship the Son of God who was born as a little baby for us, and we worship God who was willing to send his Son. Come to worship this Christmas.

God had said it long ago . . .

This talk in three parts is a reminder that God gave clues hundreds of years before the birth of Christ that he would be born. It is based on Micah 5:2. You may want to make it more visual by having the three key words (Place, Person, Past) on large cards or projected on to a screen, and move around as you speak.

Part 1

Place

'Bethlehem Ephrathah, you are one of the smallest towns in Judah . . . ' Isn't it amazing that at least 700 years before Mary and Joseph made their way from Nazareth to

Joseph's family town of Bethlehem God had planned that the birth would take place there! Micah wrote a few words of encouragement for a nation that kept turning away from God and getting themselves in a mess. Through the words that Micah said to the people and wrote down God offers some hope for them, making clear that he had not forgotten them and that a small town, less important than most places, would be where the exciting birth would take place. So it was that, at the time when Mary was nearly ready to give birth, all the people had to return to their family home towns and cities to be recorded in a big count of all people. Thousands of people would have headed for Jericho or Jerusalem, the big places, and hundreds swamped the unimportant town called Bethlehem, including the unborn Saviour of the world. The wise men had read what Micah wrote, and they were not surprised to find the star leading them to Bethlehem. God had said it long before.

Part 2

Person

'. . . but out of you I will bring a ruler . . . ' In those times there was a lot of concern and worry about who ruled which part of the land. By the time Jesus was born the Romans occupied the land which had originally belonged to God's people. In his message God used Micah to explain that a new ruler was to come, and through a prophecy of the prophet Isaiah (Isaiah 42:1-4) God goes into more detail about the kind of ruler this new King will be. The person this King would be was to be different – born in Bethlehem, a peace-maker, and a person who would change history. Out of Bethlehem God did indeed bring a ruler . . . who rules our lives with his love. God had said it long before.

Part 3

Past

'. . . whose family line goes back to ancient times.' It is hard for us to really understand how important 'family past' was in the days this was written, and the days 700 years later when Jesus was born. Most people could trace their family history back hundreds of years, and even their names gave away a little of which original clan and family their ancestors had belonged to. In those times family history and past meant everything, and Joseph, the initially unwilling husband of Mary, was from one of the oldest families, descended directly from the shepherd boy, musician and king, David. This gave the baby a royal history, and made him special. Even that detail was known to God so many years before, and all went to make the story complete. God had said it long before.

Step by step

Each step of the road through Advent has challenges. This talk is best told if the whole group, or at least some of them, could take steps for each section.

Step one

(Take one step.) The most difficult thing for Mary was to believe what the angel was telling her, and take the step forward (take one step) to trusting God. She was shocked to see an angel, and then shocked by the news that the angel said to her. She didn't know the news was coming, and she must have been very shocked. But she knew that God loved her and would be with her to help her through whatever happened, so she took that step forward (take one step) and offered herself to God.

God calls us to take a step forward too (take one step). Mary realised that her relationship with God was the most important thing in her life. For us to take a step forward (take one step) during Advent we need to learn to put God first in our lives. Our relationship with God, made possible though Jesus, must be more important than all of the festivities and attractions of the season. Only then will we step forward (take one step) during Advent.

Step two

(Take two steps.) The Advent road led Mary to the stable. The journey was not an easy one, as she is likely to have walked all the way, step by step (take two steps). As she and Joseph walked along the hot, rocky and dusty roads they must have had plenty to think about. As they slept in the cold of the night they must have continued to think through all that was happening to them. Joseph must have stepped forward (take two steps) thinking about the angel who visited him and told him to marry Mary, and Mary must have stepped forward (take two steps) thinking about all the possibilities and challenges the future would hold. As they stepped forward (take two steps) with thoughts, concerns and questions in their minds, they still kept on going.

There are plenty of distractions to stop us stepping forward during Advent (take two steps). There is so much to do, and so many people to see. There are extra meetings, lunches, dinners, celebrations and services. There are presents to buy and food to prepare. We may even have worries about the coming Christmas celebrations because they remind us of sad times or hard times in the past. To step forward (take two steps) it is important to think about these things, but not let them take over the place God should have in our lives. So as we walk the Advent road we must step forward (take two steps) and keep the real meaning of the season in our hearts and minds.

Light

There are many lights in the stories of Advent and Christmas. How do those lights, and the light of the world, help us? For this talk it would be helpful to have the following lights available at the front, held up by some volunteers: candles, large stars, lanterns, a large sun.

Advent is a time to think about light. Light is really important in our lives, especially at this time of year when the weather is dull and the darkness of night seems to begin early. We need light to show us the way on our journeys, and we need proper light so that we can enjoy our homes and families. Light makes us feel good, and it gives us a feeling of warmth. If we are feeling unsure light gives us a sense of hope. If we are heading somewhere the lights of our destination encourage us to keep going. Light is really important.

The lights of the village of Nazareth were left behind, and the two people, Mary and Joseph, walked on under the light of the sun. As the heat beat down upon them and made the dust seem hot under their feet Mary and Joseph kept on going because they had the light of God's love inside them. They had both met with God's messengers, and they had both felt the light of God change their minds and turn them to him. It would not have been an easy walk, and Mary, already heavy carrying the unborn child, must have seen the light from the sun as a danger. She had to keep going, and she did. Their final night sleeping under the night sky must have been a good one, as in the distance they saw the lights of the candles and lanterns in the streets of Bethlehem. They knew that the end of the journey was at last close, and the candle lights gave them encouragement and warmth.

The lights in the sky from stars shone over the lands in the east, the lands where the wise men lived. But one particular light in the sky, one very special star, shone brighter than the others and seemed somehow to have a life of its own. This star showed the wise men the route they should take on their journey to the birth of the Christ. By day they went carefully and slowly, looking out for any sign of the star

Talks

light. At night, with their lanterns in their hands as they rode their camels, they enjoyed the clear light that the star gave them. The light was there, moving them forward daily and leading them to the candle lights of the palace of King Herod, and then on to the lanterns in the stable in Bethlehem where the light of the world was born.

The darkness of the fields above the warm glow of the candles of Bethlehem were lit here and there by the lanterns of the shepherds. Though tired and cold, they sat and listened carefully, trying to spot the approach of any wild animals that would cause harm to their sheep. But as they watched they noticed a slight glow in the sky which got brighter and brighter, and they heard strange sounds, a little like a huge choir. They were dazzled by the light, and as they blinked made out the form of an angel, who told them not to fear but to celebrate the birth of a new Saviour of the world. As they watched, stunned and amazed, they heard the angels tell them to go down to the town and find the new baby. They grabbed their lanterns as the light in the sky faded, and dashed down to the stable as quickly as their feet would carry them.

Mary and Joseph saw the light of the sun, and the lights of the candles in Bethlehem. The wise men followed the light of the special star that carried them from their homes in the east to Jesus. The shepherds saw the amazing, dazzling light of the angels and ran towards the candlelight of the town where the baby was born.

Do we see the light? We see the light of sunshine, candles, modern lamps and light fittings, and even the far-away stars. But Advent is time to try to see and feel as better light. In the darkness of winter, and the darkness of our lives, do we want to experience the light that Jesus brings? As he spoke to a crowd Jesus described himself as the light of the world, and that includes us. Like the Wise Men, shepherds, and even the parents Mary and Joseph, this Advent we can experience the light of Jesus in our hearts.

Just a normal night

The shepherds were working in the fields on what was for them just a normal night, when amazing things happened. The response 'Just a normal night' can be used after you say 'It was . . .' or, later, 'It wasn't . . .'

The shepherds trudged up the hillside in the early evening, just as the sun was beginning to set, and it was *just a normal night*. There were the sheep grazing in the fields, and the shepherds chatted as they made for their flocks. 'Well, I need a quiet night tonight,' said one, 'I didn't get a wink of sleep today. It's so busy down in the town with that census going on.'

'Yep, I agree,' replied another, clutching his lantern as the sky got darker. 'I'm glad to be out of it for the night!' Up on the hillsides amongst their sheep it was *just a normal night*. They counted the flocks, and made sure they were all safe. They checked them over to make sure they were all fit and hadn't come to any harm during the day. The shepherds settled down, watching and listening carefully for any signs of wild animals. It was *just a normal night*.

Time passed quickly for the shepherds. They talked a little, watched the sheep resting, and one by one saw the lights in the town of Bethlehem go out as people settled to sleep in their homes. It was *just a normal night*. By the early hours of the morning it was colder, and apart from an unusual star over in the distance, everything was unchanged from how it was every night. In fact it was *just a normal night* . . . until one of the shepherds said quietly: 'Strange glow in the sky over there.' They all turned to look while the sheep stood and shook themselves as the light got brighter and brighter, like nothing they had ever seen before. 'I don't like the look of this!' one shepherd shouted above the noise of beating wings, and they all stood and stared in fear, frozen to the spot where they stood. 'Do not be afraid,' said a strange voice, calming yet with power, and out of the bright light came a figure. It wasn't *just a normal night*, now! The shepherds gasped as they listened to this amazing creature, this angel. First he explained that they should be happy because God was sending good news to them and to all people in the form of a newborn baby. Then they listened to what sounded like hundreds of wonderful voices in the most amazing choir singing praise to God. It wasn't *just a normal night*!

Once the light had faded, the singing had stopped and the angels had gone it was *just a normal night* again . . . but not for those shepherds! After making sure their sheep were safely in the sheep pens they grabbed their lanterns and ran off down the lanes back to Bethlehem to find the new-born baby. For them it wasn't *just a normal night* . . . they had been changed, and so had the world.

Just a normal night . . . just a normal season of Advent . . . just a normal Christmas . . . just a normal month . . . just a normal celebration. For the shepherds things would never be the same again because they had been changed. Let's make this Advent different – let God change you.

Put aside

This talk is based on a few verses from Ephesians 4:22 onwards, as we are encouraged to put aside things of the world and concentrate on all that God offers to us.

Part 1

The stories of Advent and Christmas are full of challenge for us. So many people had to put aside their own feelings or thoughts, plans and hopes. Let's look at two of them:

Joseph hoped to be able to get out of an embarrassing situation. He had promised to marry Mary, but had later discovered that she was going to have a baby that was not his. He knew what the gossips would be saying, and he knew that she appeared to have done wrong. But Joseph was visited in a dream by an angel, who told him to stay with Mary and who explained that the baby was special, and would save people. Joseph had to put aside all that he feared, all that he thought, and all that he felt. He had to put aside his hopes and his doubts, and follow God's plan.

Mary was rightly shocked and scared when the angel Gabriel came to her, and even more so when she heard what he had to say. She was a quiet young girl from a good family, and had been planning to marry Joseph. As she listened to the angel's words she must have imagined all her dreams going up in smoke. What would happen to the man she loved – Joseph – once he found out? What about everyone in the village, once they saw that she was expecting a child? What about the normal joy and excitement of looking forward to having children, and the hopes she wanted to have for the child? As she quietly promised to obey God's will for her, she put aside all those things, and allowed God to take control.

Part 2

So what do the actions of Joseph and Mary have to teach us this Advent? Ephesians 4:22 encourages us to: 'Put aside your old self, which made you live as you used to.' Advent is a time to put aside all that gets in the way of us obeying God's plan for our lives. As we rush around this month there are plenty of things that we need to put aside, and those things will be different for all of us. For some of us we need to put aside the greed and desire of the season, with everyone wanting more and no one really being satisfied. For others we need to put aside the things that we think make us happy, like food or drink. Yet more of us need to put aside our own hopes and desires based on selfishness rather than our need, and focus on God. What are you going to put aside this Advent?

Kneel down

It is significant that rich and powerful wise men and humble, hard-working shepherds were all willing to kneel to worship Jesus. How willing are we to kneel?

Most of us don't kneel down a great deal! Have a brief discussion with those around you about when you kneel down, why you kneel down, and who you would kneel down to.

I wonder who knelt down to the wise men back in their homeland where they probably had great wealth and power? I guess their servants knelt down to them, bowed when seeing them, and went quickly to do what they were ordered. They may have been kings or rulers, where all the people in their country or territory were expected to kneel in their presence. But it is hard to imagine that the wise men knelt down to anyone. They wouldn't need to kneel to those more powerful than them, because there wasn't anyone more powerful than them! Yet they gave up all their power and comfort to follow the star and after their long and tiring journey over many days and many miles, to kneel down before a baby born in a cold, dirty stable.

In Isaiah 45:23 there is a promise and a prophecy – God promises that the time will come when everyone everywhere will kneel to him and worship him. 'My promise is true, and it will not be changed. I solemnly promise by all that I am: everyone will come and kneel before me and vow to be loyal to me.' A time will come when all people will realise that there is nothing more worthwhile to worship than God.

I wonder what we kneel before this Advent? Do we kneel before the things that are really special to us – perhaps our homes or our cars? Do we kneel and worship all the money, present-buying and trimmings of the season? Do we kneel before the hopes we have for a good time with the family? Or do we kneel before God? If it was good enough for the rich and powerful wise men, it should be good enough for us.

Talks

Advent 1, 2, 3

This talk reminds us of the relationship between Elizabeth and Mary, and therefore between John the Baptist and Jesus Christ. For this, each time one of the numbers is said, the group can respond by holding up the appropriate number of fingers and shouting out the number.

There was one young lady who had recently got engaged to a man called Joseph. She didn't know what God's one big plan for her life was until she was visited by an angel who told her she would give birth to a special baby. A short journey away were two people who were very special to Mary, the one young lady. The two people were her older cousin Elizabeth, and her husband Zechariah. Mary went to visit the two of them, and all three celebrated God's goodness. Elizabeth and Zechariah were old and had given up the hope of having one child, let alone two or three. But they had been stunned and excited by the news that Elizabeth was going to have one after all. The two of them had been really amazed by the news. As the three people – Mary, Elizabeth and Zechariah – sat and talked Mary shared with the other two the amazing news that she was going to have a special baby. Elizabeth and Zechariah already new that their one son, who they had been told to name John, would be special. They now knew that the son who Mary would give birth to would be an even more special child – he would be the one promised, the Messiah, the Son of God.

One by one the days passed, and soon John was born. He would grow up to be a great man, and to prepare people's hearts and minds to hear what Jesus had to say. Then the child number two, Jesus, was born in the stable. John and Jesus were cousins, and as the three wise men and one large group of shepherds came to visit the two parents Mary realised how good God's plan was. Her son Jesus' cousin would be the one to get people ready for him.

We may look upon the stories of Advent and Christmas, and think that they all happened accidentally. But God had planned it to be that way, and made it look as easy as one, two, three! God's plan was good. What has God got planned for you this Advent? Can you see God's plan for your life? Are you open to God's plan?

A is for Advent

There are many words connected with the Advent season which begin with A. These 'A' words can be used as the basis for individual talks, in a series of assemblies or services, all together.

A – Anticipated

The birth of Jesus was anticipated in the writings and words of God's messengers many hundreds of years before. We can still read the anticipation in the words of the prophets Isaiah and Micah, telling of a new King who would be born, and even anticipating the town where the birth would take place, Bethlehem. Some people anticipated that the promised leader would be a strong warrior, while others thought he would be a man of peace.

A – Adventure

The whole experience was an adventure for the wise men. They had been used to power and control, and probably enjoyed real comfort and security. To leave all that behind because of some old writings and a strange star in the sky was quite an adventure. The adventure got stronger when they visited a confused and angry King Herod, and more exciting still when they found Jesus and knelt before him.

A – Aches

Have you ever been for a long walk on a dusty, stony track in the heat of the sun? Mary and Joseph had to walk for a few days to make their way from their home village of Nazareth to the town of Bethlehem so that Joseph could be added to the lists of people being counted at that time. They probably walked all the way, with Joseph carrying their clothes and bags with all that they could manage, and Mary struggling on, knowing that the baby was due at any time. There is little wonder that they were keen to rest their aching limbs in whatever place they could find, even the stable.

A – Astonished

That's just one of many words that could be used to describe the shocked and stunned surprise of the shepherds on the hillside. First it was the dazzling light, then the strange and powerful message of an angel who spoke to them. Then they were astonished by the choir, and astonished by finding this very special baby having just been born in a stable and wrapped in a cloth. The whole experience was Astonishing.

A – Angels

There are a number of angels in the Advent stories. There was the angel called Gabriel, who had the duty of telling Mary that she was to be the mother of the son of God. Then there was the angel who visited Joseph in a dream and encouraged him to stick with Mary, to care for her, and to love her and the special child Jesus. And then there were the amazing angels – perhaps too many to count – who visited the hillside above Bethlehem to tell the shepherds the good news about the birth of Jesus.

A – Awesome

What was it that made the wise men kneel at the side of the manger and leave precious, expensive gifts? The baby Jesus probably didn't look any different from any other new-born baby, yet for them this was an awesome sight and an awesome moment. They had been led there by a star in the sky, and they knew in their hearts that this little baby would change the world. For Mary and Joseph, as they welcomed the wise men and watched them worship their son, this was also quite awesome. Mary continued to wonder about it and think it all through.

A – And . . .

And what now? We know the stories, we know that Advent is about getting ready to welcome Jesus again, and we know that God sent his Son to be born in that dirty, smelly place. And so it is up to us – we either let ourselves get all wrapped up in the fuss we all make over Christmas, or we are different and allow God to lead us, like the shepherds and wise men, to worship that awesome child.

Prayers

The Advent season is one where it is important to be quiet and both speak and listen to God. On the Advent road, as we continue to think of the journeys made to reach the stable, we too can approach in prayer and quiet, and worship the Son of God. These prayers can be used on their own, in groups, to supplement Common Worship, or adapted to suit every situation.

Opening sentences

Glory to God in heaven, and peace to all people on earth.
(Luke 2:14)

Bethlehem, you are an unimportant place, but out of you will come a special leader.
(Micah 5:2)

Here is my servant, who I have chosen and have given strength.
(Isaiah 42:1)

Peace be with you! The Lord is with you and is giving you great things.
(Luke 1:28)

There is nothing that God cannot do.
(Luke 1:37)

Go – you will find the baby wrapped in strips of cloth and lying in a manger.
(Luke 2:12)

A woman will have a son and he will be called 'God with us'.
(Matthew 1:23)

In our homes

In our homes and families
God promises comfort and peace
In our churches and schools
God promises comfort and peace
In our work and our fun
God promises comfort and peace
In our excitement and anticipation
God promises comfort and peace
In our own journey through Advent
God promises comfort and peace

Feeling God's presence

Mary felt God's presence,
Holy Spirit, rest on me.
Joseph was changed by a message,
Holy Spirit, rest on me.
The wise men knew who they worshipped,
Holy Spirit, rest on me.

Preparing ourselves

It is time to prepare ourselves.
The Light of the World is coming to us.
It is time to find peace.
The Light of the World is coming to us.
It is time to give up our darkness.
The Light of the World is coming to us.
It is time to follow the light.
The Light of the World is coming to us.
We are the people who are called to serve you.
We are your people – lead us to you, Jesus.
We are the people who look for your light in this world.
We are your people – lead us to you, Jesus.
We are the people called to take your light to others.
We are your people – lead us to you, Jesus.
We are the people who should celebrate you, not the world.
We are your people – lead us to you, Jesus.

Glory to God

The angels sang the song for all the world to hear:

Glory to God in the highest, and peace on earth to all.

The shepherds heard their words, which took away their fear:

Glory to God in the highest, and peace on earth to all.

The angels celebrated the wonderful birth:

Glory to God in the highest, and peace on earth to all.

God of heaven had visited earth:

Glory to God in the highest, and peace on earth to all.

Help us to look to you

When we see the bright lights,

the decorations and the attractions

Help us to keep our eyes looking to you.

When we see the presents,

the wrappings and bows

Help us to keep our eyes looking to you.

When we see the concerts,

pantomimes and performances

Help us to keep our eyes looking to you.

When we see the cross,

the bread and the wine

Help us to keep our eyes looking to you.

We thank you, God

We have so many things to thank you for.

Thank you, God, for our joy.

We have so many feasts to look forward to.

Thank you, God, for our joy.

We have so much fun coming our way.

Thank you, God, for our joy.

We have so many gifts waiting for us.

Thank you, God, for our joy.

We have a leader to love and to follow.

Thank you, God, for our joy.

Prayers

We bring good news

May we echo the words of the angels
as we serve those around us who are lonely or sad:
Don't be afraid – we bring good news.
May we echo the words of the angels
as we meet those near who are lost and confused:
Don't be afraid – we bring good news.
May we echo the words of the angels
as we reach out to those who need a helping hand:
Don't be afraid – we bring good news.

We meet Jesus everywhere

Even the parties and celebrations can't beat this:
It's going to be great – we are going to meet Jesus.
Even the family gatherings and precious time together
don't thrill us as much:
It's going to be great – we are going to meet Jesus.
Even the presents waiting to be opened don't come close:
It's going to be great – we are going to meet Jesus.
Even every exciting event and meal put together aren't as good:
It's going to be great – we are going to meet Jesus.

I put it all aside

This Advent I put aside my selfish hopes and desires,
I put aside all that is not right.
This Advent I put aside my worries and doubts,
I put aside all that is not right.
This Advent I put aside my parties and excesses,
I put aside all that is not right.
This Advent I put aside my busyness and noise,
I put aside all that is not right.
This Advent I put aside all that stops me seeing you,
I put aside all that is not right.

We kneel and worship

We kneel before you and we worship.

As the shepherds heard the news, and rushed to see you,

We kneel before you and we worship.

As the wise men travelled for many miles to see your face,

We kneel before you and we worship.

As you call us to be different and put you at the centre of Advent,

We kneel before you and we worship.

I come before you, Jesus

I want this Advent to be special – help me make some time.

I want to see Jesus, to kneel, and to worship.

I want this Advent to be holy – help me to find the space.

I want to see Jesus, to kneel, and to worship.

I want this Advent to be moving – help me to feel your spirit.

I want to see Jesus, to kneel, and to worship.

I want this Advent to be different – help me to change.

I want to see Jesus, to kneel, and to worship.

Help me walk the Advent road

As you helped Mary and Joseph

as they walked the path that took them to the stable and the manger,

So help me, God, to walk the Advent road.

As you guided the wise men

as they followed the star that took them to the stable and the manger,

So help me, God, to walk the Advent road.

As you inspired the shepherds,

as they ran down the path that took them to the stable and the manger,

So help me, God, to walk the Advent road.

Prayers

Lord, forgive us

We have allowed ourselves to be swept along with the world
and forgotten how to live lives that are different.
Lord forgive us, and help us look to you.
We have had our heads turned by the decorations,
the spending, the fuss and the presents.
Lord forgive us, and help us look to you.
We have forgotten what it is all about,
and feel emptiness inside our souls.
Lord forgive us, and help us look to you.

We have lost our way

We have lost our way on the journey to your stable.
Lord Jesus, make us more ready to worship you.
We have taken steps which have led us away.
Lord Jesus, make us more ready to worship you.
We have not given you the time you deserve.
Lord Jesus, make us more ready to worship you.
We have forgotten what this time is for.
Lord Jesus, make us more ready to worship you.

Shine your light

Son of God, as we look to the time when the great Light of Life came
into the world we also look at ourselves.
We see darkness, failure and sadness in our hearts,
but the light of Jesus, which shone so brightly for the world to see,
can shine on us too.
Shine on us with your light, and make us right again.

We prepare

We are preparing for the coming of Jesus.

We are preparing our homes.

We are preparing our hearts.

We are preparing for the coming of Jesus.

We look ahead

Let us imagine the joys that we will know over the coming weeks.

Let us imagine the sights and sounds we will experience.

Let us imagine the smiles, the kindness, and the laughter.

Let us imagine ourselves reaching Jesus and meeting him afresh.

When we fail to understand

Lord Jesus, we fail to understand so much of your greatness.

We fail to understand why you were born into our world.

We fail to understand why you love us.

We fail to understand why you offer us so much.

Lord Jesus, we thank you.

Responses for Intercessions

During this Advent shine your light on us.

Jesus, come to us as you came to our world.

May we kneel and worship you.

Lord in your love, hear what we ask.

Jesus, born in that stable, hear us.

As we prepare to meet you, help us, we pray.

In this darkness may your light shine bright.

We ask you to come to us and help us.

Change your world, change your people, change me.

Prayers

Endings

May the love of God who sent his Son
Go with us as we prepare to meet him.

God goes with us on our journey.
Let us walk with him.
God leads us to the Saviour, Jesus.
Let us go to meet him.

There is more on the path of Advent for us to find,
may we all discover more every step.

We are walking the Advent road,
lead us to your Son.

In this time of peace,
may peace be at the centre of our lives.

Let us go to find the Christ.
Let us go to meet the Christ.
Let us go to lead others to the Christ.

God lead us to himself.
God lead us to his Son.
God lead us to his future.

Step by step may we walk God's way
this Advent, this Christmas, and every day.

May the God who sent his Son be alongside us.
May the Son who we want to meet be with us.
And may the Spirit who helps us see reveal all to us.

God go with us and bring us his peace
this Advent time, and all time.

We will walk the way of Christ.
We will go to the stable.
We will go to the cross.